Striking Light from Ashes

poems by

Charise M. Hoge

Finishing Line Press
Georgetown, Kentucky

Striking Light from Ashes

Copyright © 2017 by Charise M. Hoge
ISBN 978-1-63534-256-7 First Edition
All rights reserved under International and Pan-American Copyright Conventions.
No part of this book may be reproduced in any manner whatsoever without written permission from the publisher, except in the case of brief quotations embodied in critical articles and reviews.

ACKNOWLEDGMENTS

Liam Wilkinson published "Craft" in *Englyn* Literary Journal, April 2016 issue. David Lehman published "Entranced" on November 8, 2016, and Angela Ball published "Wash" on July 14, 2015, in Lehman's poetry column "Next Line, Please" of *The American Scholar*. The first stanza of "Making a Comeback," inspired by jazz great Ornette Coleman, and the third stanza of "Her Hourglass a Prism," a sestina, are also published in "Next Line, Please" as part of a collaborative work. Robert Lee Brewer selected the poem "Jaded" as one of the winners of his April 2016 Poem A Day challenge, published March 21, 2017 in his blog "Poetic Asides" of *Writer's Digest*.

My gratitude goes to the poets Liam Wilkinson, David Lehman, Angela Ball, Robert Lee Brewer, and Red Hawk, who have been instrumental in supporting the writing and sharing of my poetry.

Special thanks to poets Red Hawk and Robert Lee Brewer for taking on the task of reading my manuscript prior to publication and offering their wonderful endorsements.

And I am so fortunate to have met Rahela Majidi, the artist who graciously shares her painting on the cover.

Publisher: Leah Maines
Editor: Christen Kincaid
Cover Art: Rahela Majidi, http://Facebook.com/RahelArts
Author Photo: Charles Hoge
Cover Design: Elizabeth Maines McCleavy

Printed in the USA on acid-free paper.
Order online: www.finishinglinepress.com
also available on amazon.com

Author inquiries and mail orders:
Finishing Line Press
P. O. Box 1626
Georgetown, Kentucky 40324
U. S. A.

Table of Contents

Dowager's Hump 1

Oh Orlando 2

Canticle 3

Emanation 4

When Fairy Tales End 5

Fabrication 6

Cricket Cage 7

Forget the Rain 8

Her Hourglass a Prism 9

Fixtures 11

Jaded 12

in Lost River 13

Maybe 14

Entranced 15

Craft 16

Making a Comeback 17

Salvage 19

Wash 20

Boots 21

Homing 22

Knocked 23

For
the friends, family, and strangers
who inhabit these pages

Sister Muse!
Come back
with the
Spring Flowers
to dissipate
old Sorrow

—Viên Thức
monk, artist, poet

Dowager's Hump

With a bent verticality
she carries and carries
what may have started
as an apple—the one that framed
her, that she's ordained to swallow
—or what may have begun
as a seed that burrowed
into her yielding
as she knows how to field
a demand, how to shoulder
an equation that doesn't add up,
how to solidify her bloodstream
while winds are raging;
and when she crosses the street
old and withered
you see that Atlas was a woman.

Oh Orlando

Give them a soft landing
into the aprons
of the ones who
fed the mothers of the mothers
of these stricken does.

Gather them into the cloth
that brushed the brow
of the children who labored
for the children who bore them.

Sway them with the sweat
of a better future
which suddenly belongs to us.

Canticle

Peace is hard to find when no one's looking.
There's no kingdom or valley where it stays.
Encased in the ugly face of a reckoning,
peace is hard to find when no one's looking.
A beacon caught between our believing,
a hum behind the tune that's overplayed,
peace is hard to find when no one's looking.
There's no kingdom or valley where it stays.

Emanation

perhaps the exactness of lichen imbues
damp woods to celebrate in hues
of mushrooms: magenta, citrine,
laurel green
untrammel the eye

as I
have evaded
the masquerade
of our capitol's Fourth of July
for the staccato flare of fireflies
set against mountains rise and rest
where dark air has no blankness

When Fairy Tales End

There are words unborn,
not even shed, inchoate, unsaid;

within reach,
squeezed between toes,
curled into anonymity.

Trampling my sole/soul,
stumbling into the errant girl
who would name me.

A wraith, she waits,
not for an awakening kiss
of a prince;
but for the timbre of her voice
in my throat.

Fabrication

A green scarf
looped across your waist,
tied at the side
as an exclamation point.
It set me spinning.

Where? I asked
are you going?
You said,
matter of factly,
dance class.

We were four.
I was allowed outdoors
in front of the house
or behind the house,
with my sister to the end of the street,
with my family in the car.

How the ends of that emerald tulle
t-r-a-i-l-e-d when you skipped,
a trail I followed… over the streets
past the cars out of the city
to the sea,
like a shimmery net
with ebb and flow
of cadency,
the deep green folds
billowing with treasures.

Yes,
my mother said,
I could go too.

Cricket Cage

funny story how a cricket got caught in the wax of our candle
in our other apartment,
the one we left because the heat never worked properly
and the landlady didn't listen,
the laughter we shared for warmth about the sticking cricket
the laughter that coaxed us out of that place
as we emptied our quarters secretly
since our lease still had time on it
and the landlady didn't see
we moved into the city proper
where the whim of the moment is easily satisfied
where everything is nearby
and I bought a cricket cage that has no function
except to resonate
the delight we found in the cold of our living room

Forget the Rain

It's a constant complaint,
beating down like an answer
to an unasked question,
like an insult to a picnic,
a hesitation to venture.

This clerk, who has adopted America,
says it's a blessing
… and you remember the dry spell
from your rear view mirror.
How you acted as guardian
of the thirsty garden,
beholden to unseen mouths of roots.
You remember the parchedness,
the fierce need, as he tells you
to have a good day.

Her Hourglass a Prism

Moored in the hospital, May titles her book:
How to Leave Port
in a Tethered Dress.
Startled bystanders will launch songs
as she takes the plunge without fear,
royalties paid in currency of spirit.

An attic houses her wedding dress
—unruffled, this vision of import
keeps vigil by her bed, appears as a lack of fear.
She hears the vows that bind spirits,
lending to an ever after, amending end of book.
"In the tenor of a voice once mine is a song."

Visitors spark with lyrics of ballads, of songs,
a lamentation for the lack of redress
to tip the scale of slippery life. She jests, "Book
me a room with a courtyard and easy transport."
A smile dawns on her lips this cup won't pass; her spirit
a salve on tarnished will, her winsome style to balk at fear.

Taut her sail against the curve of fear,
medical chart swerves off course. Songs
of Sirens seeking to engulf her spirit,
steer her head, her prowess dressed
in white sheet billowing breath—no safe port
but the touch of sterile things and treasured books.

Is this just—what if she throws out the book,
starts a second career of needling fear,
designs plans for another year, deports
her foreign cells to a singular song
that lasts as long as an epitaph, dresses
in heels to reveal her elevated spirit?

May has a panacea of ingredients for a free spirit:
abandon bookish traits to be an open book,
trash the travail of perfect fitted dress, and address
aspirations adrift in the guise of fear.
The drum of her heels echoes, the hum of her song
catches on. She departs by portal to a pier without a port.

See the comport of her spirit
buoyed by song, in her notebook:
"Dear fear, our demise is just an ill-fitting dress."

Fixtures

There is a forgotten god
of Greek mythology.

The one who keeps
the unimportant things
in place:

pictures in frames,
spices under lids of jars,
letters ensconced in drawers.

The one who rests on my sofa,
with smiling beatitude holds the floor.

He is undisturbed
while my plans fail,
expectations sifted out
of the contents
of the day's catch.

This god caresses
a still life with pleasure.

Jaded

Somewhere
in the heart of harm
I want to sweep you
off your calloused feet,
your callousness nestling
in a hyacinth wreath
—drunk on spring
perfuming the crevices
where love rots,
where cradles splinter,
to unearth the eager
crook of your arm.

in Lost River

nature speaks
without vocabulary
without tense
and when I listen
my thoughts
shift out of sequence,
pieces of a puzzle displaced,
in the wake of

moss more green than
green
trail soft with ancient
respect
the woman tree with knots of breasts
holding court
over the salient spring feeding into
our pond
next to this flat rock
set with stones for each visit
we made here
you placed one stone upon
leaving
all your child years
given back to me

again

Maybe

…it was a false start
…an orchestra warming up
…warble seeking wings
…downbeat without a measure
it was never a mistake

Entranced
> *"I prefer the sign 'No Entry' to the one that says 'No Exit'."*
> —*Stanislaus Lec*

Here he goes showing up
so she's hanging on,
trapped as a trapeze
in swing, between goodbyes.

His hello is wide—
she's soft for a lofty welcome
(unpracticed in soft landings).
He has her in suspense. If
she reads and heeds the signs,
they all shine 'Going Nowhere'.

Craft

Spew a gem, whole in hue.
Burnished facets of clarity
furnish the layout of her lines,
mined from the muck she's in.

Making a Comeback

The trip begins without a sign that's hung.
The mark may lie within your palm a line
a psychic knew before your time was sung.
She saw the span of dissonance: you pine
to scale a chart, depart where others clung;
refuse the map, forget reviews unkind.
My year of birth your cry of "Something Else!!!!"
A gypsy soul keeps nothing on the shelf.

The ride's not smooth, the border is askew.
One note will find another that redeems
a melody the organ grinder knew.
And few took heed of Joshua Bell, it seems,
when he picked up his violin on cue
beside the metro. Caravan of dreams
will camp on city streets when stars align.
Such constellations shift my paradigm.

The rubble of the days that went off track
derail the road for rugged tapestry.
A thread will weave a tale that has the knack
to detour from predictability.
So raise the tempo with your band to back
me up, embark on the exploratory.
Terrain runs out; then follow the tune of raw
unguarded moments, pause rewinding flaws.

A tangent season suddenly thudded
like heavy cloaks now soaked no longer warming.
We bristled to the corners of the bed.
My pulse decried the effort of a drumming
for steadiness—to improvise instead.
Rephrase the clash unwieldy from repeating.
Exchange the forgery of fallen leaves
for murmur amplified upon the breeze.

Hibiscus bloom deserts its host, descends
below, falsetto tones cascading there.
A praying mantis my repining rends
unnecessary. Restlessness of air
lends sound of saxophone around a bend
…where I am sleeping in a shelter. Ere
the break of day I'll rest a thousand nights
off pavement sheets, by forte rise to write.

Salvage

There isn't anything
to throw away.
Gamble on brokenness
of edges—
which were your pillars,
useless except to fixate you—
and you're malleable as mercy.
Wing it after the burn out.
Some Phoenix-like dawn
will draw a dedication
from your tepid, tender pulse.

Wash

No perfumes or dyes, for sensitive skin.
May irritate eyes, keep from reach of children.
Sorting serves to distort the all at once-ness:
lifting covers for a yet to be known lover,
tugging at last season's pants, button hole evaded,
folding up one thought to air another,
eyeing a secretly passed note pocketed
in shorts—saying it's time for a willowy
daughter to do her own laundry.

Boots

There's a thunder
in her heels,
like a proud flamenco woman
she's harnessed her ovarios,
balls of moon
to oscillate her turf,
sling her daughters
upon the cresting
deliverance of a "no
—no, I will not sit
upon your lap"
(pretty as a lamp
with a burned out bulb).
She's risen
in fuchsia and brown kickers
setting sparks
that will do
for an "I do"
as she scuffs the floor
of conciliation
with her grit of
serving divorce.

Homing

Could it be there were three
migrant angels? One at your head,
one to cradle your feet, and one
to hover at your quiet body
not quite complete
with us, your children, grandchildren,
and these tempests of illness.
I read to you;
you couldn't object.
I reckoned with death,
imminent suitor
who would win you over.
And three sorrys
I said, unrehearsed
—as you ditched the ward
for a bench outside,
where the long tumult settles
amongst the azaleas
and we have no need to dwell
…on what could have been better.

Knocked

Whereby resentment,
stepsister to resilience
(sidesteps, sidesteps apart),
becomes a wall retaining
tidiness, against the turning
tide, the trying start.

And what will erode at last,
what will roll off a terse back
to return to the sway of the sea?
To loll, ladled on a rock like the seal,
sunning in supine vulnerability,
harmoniously salty.

Perhaps the lasting firmament
that lines fine filaments
gone taut will talk of ease,
will tell how to disagree
with the taunt of wrongs.
Unfetter something like song.

Charise M. Hoge is a graduate of Sarah Lawrence College (BA), New York University (MA, Dance Movement Therapy), and University of Georgia (Master of Social Work). Her career has always interwoven expressive arts—writing, dance, movement—with healing. She has been a company member of *PATH Dance Company*, Baltimore; *Room To Move*, Atlanta; and *Ancient Rhythms Dance*, Washington, D.C. She has worked as a dance/movement therapist with psychiatric and prison populations, as a mental health counselor for the international expatriate community of Bangkok, Thailand, and as a coach on identity and relocation. Her yoga and dance programs over the past eighteen years have included classes for staff of the World Bank, the U.S. Holocaust Memorial Museum, the National Gallery of Art, and the National Zoo.

As a writer, she co-authored *A Portable Identity: A Woman's Guide to Maintaining a Sense of Self While Moving Overseas*, and contributed her story as a military spouse for the book *Once a Warrior Always a Warrior*. Charise continues to consult, teach, perform in collaboration with dance theatre choreographers of Washington, D.C., and is devoted to writing. Her poetry appears in *Englyn Journal*, David Lehman's poetry column "Next Line, Please" of *The American Scholar* as well as the forthcoming book *Next Line, Please* (Cornell University Press), the graduate course "Arts and Healing" at Lesley University, and her poetry blog mixandmossspoetry.com.

www.ingramcontent.com/pod-product-compliance
Lightning Source LLC
LaVergne TN
LVHW041517070426
835507LV00012B/1635